Leaving My Homeland

A Refugee's Journey from Ukraine

Ellen Rodger

CRABTREE
PUBLISHING COMPANY
WWW.CRABTREEBOOKS.COM

CRABTREE
PUBLISHING COMPANY
WWW.CRABTREEBOOKS.COM

Author: Ellen Rodger

Editors: Sarah Eason, Harriet McGregor,
  Wendy Scavuzzo, and Janine Deschenes

Proofreader and indexer: Wendy Scavuzzo

Editorial director: Kathy Middleton

Design: Paul Myerscough and Jessica Moon

Cover design: Paul Myerscough and Jessica Moon

Photo research: Rachel Blount

**Production coordinator and
  Prepress technician:** Ken Wright

Print coordinator: Katherine Berti

Consultants: Hawa Sabriye and HaEun Kim, Centre for Refugee Studies,
  York University

Produced for Crabtree Publishing Company by Calcium Creative

Publisher's Note: The story presented in this book is a fictional account
based on extensive research of real-life accounts by refugees, with the aim
of reflecting the true experience of refugee children and their families.

Photo Credits:
t=Top, bl=Bottom Left, br=Bottom Right

Inside: Jessica Moon: p. 29b; Shutterstock: Shultay Baltaay: p. 17b;
Brothers Good: p. 6; DmyTo: pp. 7tl, 18b, 24r; Drop of Light: p. 15t;
Horkins: p. 19t; IgorGolovniov: p. 12tr; Ink Drop: p. 7b; Orest lyzhechka:
pp. 18t, 22b, 26-27t; Katatonia82: p. 8c; Mykola Komarovskyy:
pp. 25b, 26-27b; Denis Kornilov: p. 14r; Krivinis: p. 25t; Dmytro Larin: p.
21t; Lawkeeper: p. 27b; Macrovector: pp. 3, 19tr; MSSA: pp. 28t, 29l; Panda
Vector: p. 12t; Photoroyalty: p. 15b; Stas Ponomarencko:
p. 13t; Srdjan Randjelovic: p. 17r; Const Skomorok: p. 16; Sunflowerr:
p. 5b; VectorShow: p. 23b; Vladmark: p. 9c; Alexandr Zadiraka: p. 7tr;
Marcelian Zieba: p. 8b; © UNHCR: © UNHCR/Anastasia Vlasova:
p. 29t; Wikimedia Commons: В.Власенко: p.11t; Chernov/Unframe/
www.unframe.com/: p. 14b; Dod: p. 22t; Joshua Dodds, U.S. Army: p. 5t;
Gnesener1900: p. 20t; НОВОРОСС: p. 11c; Kagor: p. 9t.

Cover: Jessica Moon; Shutterstock: Artshock.

Library and Archives Canada Cataloguing in Publication

Rodger, Ellen, author
    A refugee's journey from Ukraine / Ellen Rodger.

(Leaving my homeland)
Includes index.
Issued in print and electronic formats.
ISBN 978-0-7787-4689-8 (hardcover).--
ISBN 978-0-7787-4700-0 (softcover).--
ISBN 978-1-4271-2073-1 (HTML)

    1. Refugees--Ukraine--Juvenile literature. 2. Refugee children--
Ukraine--Juvenile literature. 3. Refugees--Social conditions--Juvenile
literature. 4. Ukraine--Social conditions--Juvenile literature. I. Title.

HV640.5.U38R63 2018   j305.9'0691409477   C2017-907652-3
                                                     C2017-907653-1

Library of Congress Cataloging-in-Publication Data

CIP available at the Library of Congress

Crabtree Publishing Company
www.crabtreebooks.com   1-800-387-7650

Printed in the U.S.A./022018/CG20171220

Published in Canada
Crabtree Publishing
616 Welland Ave.
St. Catharines, Ontario
L2M 5V6

Published in the United States
Crabtree Publishing
PMB 59051
350 Fifth Avenue, 59th Floor
New York, New York 10118

Published in the United Kingdom
Crabtree Publishing
Maritime House
Basin Road North, Hove
BN41 1WR

Published in Australia
Crabtree Publishing
3 Charles Street
Coburg North
VIC, 3058

What Is in This Book?

Leaving Ukraine

Where would you go if fighting broke out in your country? How would you know who to trust to keep you safe? Ukraine is a country in eastern Europe. Since 2014, the eastern part of the country has been a battleground. Ukrainian government troops are fighting forces that support its neighbor, Russia.

Thousands of people have been killed or have gone missing in the **conflict**. Russia has taken control of land that used to belong to Ukraine. This region is called Crimea. Part of a Ukrainian region in eastern Ukraine, called Donetsk **Oblast**, has broken away from the country. It has declared itself **independent**.

Ukraine borders many countries and the Black Sea. Kiev is its capital. Donetsk is a city in the region of Donetsk Oblast.

Belarus

Russia

Poland

Kiev

Ukraine

Slovakia

Donetsk

Hungary

Moldova

Donetsk Oblast

Romania

Crimea

Black Sea

Turkey

UN Rights of the Child

Every child has rights. Rights are privileges and freedoms that are protected by law. **Refugees** have the right to special protection and help. The **United Nations (UN)** Convention on the Rights of the Child is a document that lists the rights of children all over the world. Think about these rights as you read this book.

This is the flag of the Donetsk region, which is now called the Donetsk People's Republic.

As part of its training, the Ukraine army practices martial arts.

Many people have left eastern Ukraine because of the fighting. They fear for their lives. Most have become **internally displaced persons (IDPs)**. This means they have moved to safer areas of the same country. Others have left Ukraine to live in Russia, or other neighboring countries. They are refugees. Refugees are people who flee their **homeland** because of unsafe conditions. Refugees are different from **immigrants**. Immigrants choose to leave to look for better opportunities in another country.

My Homeland, Ukraine

Ukraine is a country of differences. It is both old and new, and it is a mix of Eastern and Western **cultures**. Ukraine's landscape includes mountains in the west, plains in the middle, and sea coast in the south. It is the second-largest country in Europe. It shares borders with seven countries: Moldova, Romania, Hungary, Slovakia, Poland, Belarus, and Russia.

Ukraine has been home to different cultures and peoples for thousands of years. Its land was often invaded by groups from the west and east. In the late 1700s, it became part of the **Russian Empire**. In 1922, Ukraine became part of the **Union of Soviet Socialist Republics (USSR)**.

Kiev

Kiev is the capital of Ukraine.

Dnieper River

Ukraine's Story in Numbers

44.3 million
people live in Ukraine.

In 2004, Ukrainians protested against the government. They believed the election was rigged, or that its outcome was unfair.

The Donetsk People's Republic (DPR) has its own army.

After the breakup of the USSR in 1991, Ukraine again became an independent country. The new country had years of problems. There were major protests against the government. Parts of Ukraine did not want to belong to Russia or Ukraine.

The gold of the Ukrainian flag represents its fields of wheat. The blue represents its sky, mountains, and streams.

In 2013 to 2014, there was a **revolution**. The president was removed from office. Russia took control of Crimea, a part of southern Ukraine. **Pro-Russian** groups in eastern Ukraine also took control of different areas. Part of Donetsk Oblast declared independence. **Militia** groups announced that the new country would be called the Donetsk People's Republic (DPR). Ukrainian troops have been fighting the militias since 2014.

7

Miron's Story: Before the Bombs

My favorite thing about my city, Donetsk, is my football (soccer) team. They are the best. They beat all the others. It is true! They are called FC Shakhtar Donetsk... or they were before the fighting. They played at a big stadium called Donbass Arena. My father took me to matches there on my birthdays.

Donetsk is a big city in eastern Ukraine. My mother and father worked at the coal mines. My mother was an engineer, and my father worked in maintenance.

Miron's favorite football team is FC Shakhtar Donetsk (in striped shirts). Football is called soccer in North America.

Many people in Ukraine work at the coal mines.

In Donetsk, we had a nice house. We lived with my baba, which means grandmother in Russian. She was my father's mother, and was from Russia. We are both Russian and Ukrainian. My teta (great aunt) also lived with us. I have a sister, too, named Nastasiya. She does not like football, but she loves hockey and basketball.

Pampushky are fruit-filled doughnuts. They are a traditional homemade treat.

At our house, we had a big garden with fruit trees. We also had chickens in the back. Baba was the best cook. She was so good! Her pampushky were my favorite. My mouth waters just thinking of them. Baba and my aunt took care of us when my parents were working. When they were not working, we did all kinds of fun stuff. Going to FC Shakhtar Donetsk matches was the best, though.

Ukraine's Story in Numbers

This chart shows the **ethnic groups** in Ukraine.

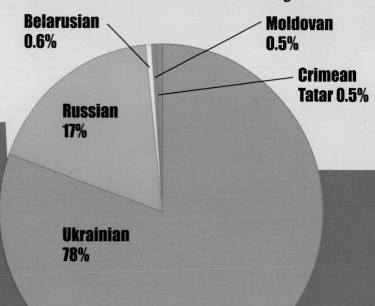

Belarusian 0.6%

Moldovan 0.5%

Crimean Tatar 0.5%

Russian 17%

Ukrainian 78%

Protests and War

Ukraine's revolution, in 2013 to 2014, was named the Euromaidan Revolution. Protesters in Kiev wanted to get rid of the president and the government. They thought the government was corrupt, or dishonest. They also believed Russia had too much power over Ukraine. People in other areas of Ukraine did not feel the same way.

Russia did not like the new Ukrainian government. It sent forces into Crimea. Most of the people in Crimea are **ethnic Russians**. Helped by Russia, local militias took control in Crimea. Crimea was later taken over by Russia.

UN Rights of the Child

The government has a responsibility to ensure that your rights are protected.

Donetsk Oblast and Luhansk Oblast are part of a larger area of Ukraine called Donbass. There, Russian supporters fought the Ukraine government.

Russia

Kiev

Ukraine

Luhansk Oblast

Luhansk

Donetsk

Donetsk Oblast

Crimea

Black Sea

People in the area of Donbass in eastern Ukraine began to protest the Ukrainian government, too. Donbass is a larger area that includes the Donetsk Oblast. Most of the people who live there are ethnic Russians. The protests turned violent, then into war. Pro-Russian militias battled against Ukrainian government forces. Russia supplied the militias with money and weapons. There were also pro-Ukrainian militias. Some of these were supported by the Ukrainian government.

Early in the war, pro-Russian militias took over many eastern cities and government buildings. Militias in the cities of Donetsk and Luhansk voted for independence from Ukraine.

The people in the cities of Donetsk and Luhansk demanded to be allowed to vote.

Miron's Story: In Hiding

When the militias first took over, it was confusing. My father was thinking we must choose a side. My mother wanted no part of war. My mother has family in Dnipro and Kiev, in western Ukraine. My mother's family wanted us to come live with them. Baba and Teta would not leave. They were born there. Baba was also sick and could not travel. Where Baba stays, Teta stays. So we all stayed.

Many buildings were destroyed by mortars, a type of bomb.

At night, bombs fell. Most of us huddled in the bathroom. We slept in the tub and on the floor. Baba and Teta stayed in their bedroom with the chickens. People had been stealing food. So, the chickens lived in the house with us. Baba said she was not afraid to die with them. But I think she was just trying to be brave for us. We were all like scared chickens when the **mortars** landed.

Apartment buildings had bullet holes and were missing parts where mortars had struck.

Our neighbor's house was turned into rubble. An apartment building two streets away was destroyed. School was closed. I was sad about that. Nastasiya was angry because she wanted to complete her studies. My parents still had to work. Sometimes, they were stranded for many days at the mines. There was a bomb shelter there and one close to our house, too.

We only went to the shelter if we had to. Mostly, Baba would not go. She was getting sicker. Her **pension** and Teta's pension payments from the government had stopped coming in. That made it hard to pay for Baba's medicines for pain.

Living Through the Conflict

War and conflict completely change everyday life. People who have jobs may lose them as factories and businesses close. Without jobs, they struggle to feed their families. The danger from bombing and bullets means schools close, too. All areas of normal life change or stop.

Just staying alive is difficult. People can be shot as they leave home to shop for food. In cities and villages, supplies are cut off when there is fighting in the streets. There is often little food available to buy. Power and water supplies are cut off as well. This makes it hard to cook, wash, or stay warm in cold weather.

This is all that is left of Donetsk airport after it was bombed.

Militias are often armed with guns. It is very dangerous to go outside.

Ukrainian president, Petro Poroshenko, visits his troops in Donetsk.

When it is more dangerous to stay than it is to leave, people flee. IDPs go to safer areas in their own country. Refugees leave for neighboring countries. In eastern Ukraine, people who had the money to leave took cars or trains to safer areas. Many traveled to Russia.

In some cases, people were not allowed to leave. The militias did not want healthy men to leave. They wanted them to join their groups and fight. Militias looked for people who they believed supported one side over the other. If the people did not share their beliefs, they were kidnapped, beaten, or killed.

Ukraine's Story in Numbers

1.7 million

people are **registered** IDPs in Ukraine.

Miron's Story: Too Dangerous to Stay

My father's cousin was kidnapped by militia that supports the Ukrainian government. He was accused of being a separatist. A separatist is someone who wants Donetsk to leave Ukraine. They beat him and demanded money from his family. His family was lucky they had some money to pay and he was allowed to go home.

After that, my father wanted us to leave. My parents were not working. We had little money and food. He arranged for us to travel to my mother's sister in Dnipro. But only my mother, my sister, and I would go. Baba was too sick to travel. And besides, my father thought he would not be allowed to leave. He stayed home to care for Baba and Teta.

Government-supporting militia kidnapped, beat, or killed anyone they thought was a separatist.

We did not want to leave, but my father said it was okay and he would join us later. He said we would be safe in Dnipro. We would have family to help. We could go to school again and sleep at night because there would be no bombing. I felt that he was lying. Nastasiya thought so, too.

When I said goodbye to Baba and Teta, Teta gave me her cross. Baba said that if Nastasiya and I worked together, the burden would not be heavy. I think that meant she wanted us to be good and to help our mother. It hurt to leave, but it was too dangerous to stay.

Homes were damaged when grenades, another type of bomb, exploded inside them.

Many Ukrainian refugees left their homes. They traveled to cities such as Dnipro, where they felt safer.

Battles and Ceasefires

There have been many ceasefires in the war in Ukraine. Ceasefires happen when the two sides agree to stop fighting. They often last for just a short time. Sometimes, ceasefires allow the sides to work on a peaceful solution to war. During ceasefires, people can leave their homes without fearing that they will be harmed. This allows them to get food, water, and medical help, or to flee to other areas.

Many families have lost loved ones.

Ceasefires allow people to leave their homes. Troops still patrol the streets, but there is no fighting.

In 2017, there were

2.6 million

Ukrainian refugees worldwide.

There have been many ceasefires in Ukraine, but the fighting continues.

About 800,000 people live near the lines of fighting in Ukraine. The fighting breaks up families. A family member may be killed. Some family members leave, while others do not or cannot leave. The poor are less likely to move in Ukraine because they have no money to travel. They also may not have anywhere to go. They may have no way to support themselves if they move.

Miron's Story: City of Refuge

When we got to my aunt's apartment, it was dark. I was tired, even though the drive to Dnipro was only 55 miles (250 km). Dnipro is a big city, even bigger than Donetsk! Compared to home, the quiet was unbelievable. There was no bombing, no gunfire, and no tanks in the streets. I did not miss the war, but I missed home. We tried to call my father many times, but could not get an answer.

Dnipro has a population of 1 million people.

There were eight of us in my aunt's apartment. My aunt and uncle shared their bedroom with my cousins Halyna and Juliya. My mother, Nastasiya, and I shared the other bedroom with my cousin Maksym.

Dnipro is a city far away from the city of Donetsk in Donetsk Oblast.

Kiev

Ukraine

Dnipro

Luhansk

Donetsk

Crimea

We were safe, but I was still scared. I hid it from my mother. Only Nastasiya could tell. When I had bad dreams, she gathered me close and told me things would be good again.

My mother thought she could get a good job in Dnipro. The city has many factories. There was even a rocket factory that employs engineers. But the rocket factory was already not paying its workers. Many people had no jobs. My mother took cleaning jobs for money. We also started school with my cousins. I liked it! Plus, my uncle and Maksym took me to an FC Dnipro match. It reminded me of going to matches with my father. I miss him so much.

Ukraine's Story in Numbers

Ukraine is among the top 10 countries in the world for numbers of people who have been internally displaced.

60,000
Russian troops are in Ukraine or along the Russian-Ukrainian border.

2,700
Ukrainian fighters have been killed.

10,000
Ukrainian fighters have been wounded.

My uncle and Maksym took me to an FC Dnipro match. FC Dnipro players wear blue.

We finally heard from my father. He said the fighting was very bad. He wanted to leave, but Baba was too sick. She had no medicine and she could not walk. He told my mother that if work did not improve for her, we should go to Kiev. There, we could live with my other aunt.

21

Where to Flee?

It is not easy for Ukrainians to find safety and a place to stay. Often, in the Donetsk and Luhansk regions, people cannot move around freely. The militias and Ukrainian army control where people can go. Fighting makes leaving too dangerous for many. Land mines are used on roads to harm enemy troops. But they also kill and injure ordinary people. Militia groups and the Ukrainian military often use people's houses as bases for fighting.

Land mines are a type of bomb that are buried underground. They explode when they are stepped on.

Hundreds of people are missing. Some of them are held by the militias. Human rights groups have said people have been beaten and killed by militias.

People mourn those who have been killed in the fighting.

By 2015, registered IDPs from eastern Ukraine were living in five main regions. The locations of unregistered IDPs are not known.

Kharkiv Oblast:
186,674 IDPs

Luhansk Oblast:
213,758 IDPs

Dnipropetrovsk Oblast:
72,391 IDPs

Zaporizhia Oblast:
99,848 IDPs

Donetsk Oblast:
539,547 IDPs

Most of the people who flee the fighting go to safer areas of their own country. IDPs can register with the government. They can apply for help with moving and housing. Those Ukrainians who have fled to neighboring countries have mostly gone to Russia. They are mostly ethnic Russians. Russia gives refugees the same rights as its citizens. However, becoming a legal refugee and being allowed to stay in Russia is a long and complicated process.

UN Rights of the Child

You have the right to be protected from being hurt in body and mind.

Miron's Story: Building a New Life

We got sad news. Baba died. My father had to make her grave in our backyard in Donetsk. He could not take her to the cemetery. The gravediggers have all left. My father and Teta are leaving, too. They are coming to live with us soon. But we do not live in Dnipro anymore. We now live in the capital city of Kiev with my aunt Olena and little cousin Nyura.

My mother found a job here. But it is not like her work before the war. Nastasiya and I walk Nyura to her school on the way to our school. Nyura's school is painted in bright colors. I think I liked my school in Dnipro better. I wish we could have stayed there. At our new school in Kiev, the kids make fun of my accent. The Ukrainian language is different from Russian. I pretend that I do not speak Russian at all. I do not want to get in any fights.

Some schools in Kiev are painted in bright, cheerful colors.

52 percent

of Ukraine's IDPs are in the Donetsk and Luhansk regions.
4 percent (62,600) are **disabled**.
13 percent (190,200) are children.
59 percent (887,800) are elderly (old) or pensioners.

More than 2.8 million people live in the capital city of Kiev.

Nastasiya says we will have a funeral for Baba when Father comes to live with us. I do not know if we can ever go back home. Even my football team, FC Shakhtar Donetsk, has left the city. The team now plays in the city of, Kharkiv, where it is safer. I am happy my family is safe, but I wish things could have been different.

When they first join a new school, it can be difficult for IDPs and refugees to fit in.

Challenges Refugees Face

Imagine losing everything and having to move to a new city or country. You have no books, toys, or perhaps nothing more than a bag of clothing. This is the reality for IDPs and refugees. Often, they must rebuild their lives from almost nothing.

IDPs in Ukraine may face **poverty** and prejudice. Prejudice is when people are treated badly because of their **race**, religion, or other unfair reasons. When people leave their homes to save their lives, they also leave behind their jobs, schools, and friends. Without a job, they cannot pay for food or housing. It is not easy to get a good job in a new city. There are often few jobs available in the **host cities** or places where IDPs live. In those places, some people think IDPs make the problems worse.

IDP families sometimes have no choice. They must rely on the government or friends and family for money.

IDPs usually stay in touch with the family members they have left behind.

The Ukraine government provides some money for IDPs who do not have jobs. It is not much. Children can go to schools where they are taught in the Ukrainian language. Ukrainian refugees in Russia are also supported by the government until they can get jobs. Children can also go to Russian-only language schools. There are Ukrainian refugees in the countries that border Ukraine. But Ukrainian refugees are not often accepted in other areas of the world.

Many IDPs and refugees feel afraid even when they are safe. Children may have nightmares or difficulty concentrating. The war may be in their past, but it still plays a part in their lives.

UN Rights of the Child

You have the right to practice your own culture, language, and religion.

You Can Help!

There are many things you can do to help newcomers and refugees in your community and elsewhere. Here are just a few ideas.

☑ Go to a library and take out books on a country, such as Ukraine, where there is conflict. Learn about the people there. You can help educate others to prevent fear and hatred.

☑ Offer to help refugees in your community. You could volunteer with an organization that assists refugees.

☑ Invite a newcomer at school to your home for dinner. Or accept an invitation to their home.

☑ Volunteer to practice speaking English with a refugee.

☑ Ask an adult to help you organize a fundraiser. It can be a lemonade stand, or used book and toy sale. Donate the money you earn to a group that helps IDPs and refugees.

☑ Take part in World Refugee Day on June 20 every year.

You have the right to food, clothing, and a safe place to live.

IDPs, like this family from Luhansk Oblast, deserve the chance to live peaceful lives.

Discussion Prompts

1. Explain the difference between a refugee, an immigrant, and an IDP.
2. Many pages in this book have boxes that list the UN Rights of the Child. What are rights? Why is it important for people to have rights?
3. How would you feel if you were an IDP and had to leave your home, friends, and family members?

Glossary

conflict Fighting

cultures The shared beliefs, values, customs, traditions, arts, and ways of life of particular groups of people

disabled Having a condition that limits someone's senses, movement, or activities

ethnic groups Groups of people who have the same ethnic or religious origin

ethnic Russians People from the countries of the former USSR

homeland The country where someone was born or grew up

host cities Cities that offer to give refugees a home

immigrants People who leave one country to live in another

independent Free from outside control

internally displaced persons (IDPs) People who are forced from their homes during a conflict but remain in their country

militia A military force made up of ordinary citizens

mortars Small missiles that are fired from a big gun

Oblast A province or region in Ukraine

pension Regular payments made to a person after they retire

poverty The state of being very poor and having few belongings

pro-Russian In favor of or supporting Russia

race People with a shared culture, history, or language

refugees People who flee from their own country to another due to unsafe conditions

registered Signed up and put on an official list

revolution The forced removal of a government or leader to completely replace them

Russian Empire A very large group of countries controlled by Russia from 1721 to 1917

United Nations (UN) An international organization that promotes peace between countries and helps refugees

Union of Soviet Socialist Republics (USSR) Until 1991, it was a large group of 15 countries, including Russia, in what is now Europe

Learning More

Books

Kent, Deborah. *Ukraine* (Enchantment of the World).
Mankato, MN: Capstone Press, 2015.

Murray, Julie. *Ukraine* (Explore the Countries Set 4). Edina, MN:
Big Buddy Books, 2017.

Stewart, Gail. *Ukraine: Then and Now* (The Former Soviet Union:
Then and Now). San Diego, CA: Referencepoint Press, 2014.

Websites

http://easyscienceforkids.com/all-about-ukraine
This site gives easy and simple information about Ukraine's geography
and people.

www.mercycorps.org/articles/ukraine/quick-facts-about-ukraine-crisis
Find out more about how ordinary people have been affected by the
problems in Ukraine.

www.unicef.org/rightsite/files/uncrcchilldfriendlylanguage.pdf
Learn more about the United Nations Convention on the Rights
of the Child.

Index

About the Author

Ellen Rodger is a descendant of refugees who fled persecution and famine. She has written and edited many books for children and adults on subjects as varied as potatoes, how government works, social justice, war, soccer, and lice and fleas.